BE WHAT YOU WISH

NEVILLE GODDARD

Paperback: 978-939057511-4

Sanage Publishing House LLP
Mumbai, India

sanagepublishing@gmail.com

Neville Lancelot Goddard generally known simply as Neville, was an American author who wrote on the Bible, mysticism, and self-help.

Neville came to the United States to study drama at the age of seventeen. During his entertaining tour in England as a vaudeville dancer and stage actor, he developed a great interest in metaphysics. Hence, he gave up his entertainment job and devote fully to the study of metaphysics and spiritual matters. Neville gives the readers the necessary tools to understand and manifest what they desire in their lives.

According to Goddard, the stories of Esau and Jacob, sons of Issac, are a metaphor of the method by which men manifest their desires.

CONTENT

INTRODUCTION

Most men are totally unaware of the creative power of imagination and invariably bow before the dictates of 'facts' and accepts life on the basis of the world without. But when you discover this creative power within yourself, you will boldly assert the supremacy of imagination and put all things in subjection to it.

It is believed that all men can change the course of their lives. By our imagination, by our affirmations, we can change our world, we can change our future. If we strive passionately to embody a new and higher concept of ourselves, then all things will be at our service.

1. BE WHAT YOU WISH

A newspaperman related to me that our great scientist, Robert Millikan, once told him that he had set a goal for himself at an early age when he was still very poor and unproven in the great work he was to do in the future. He condensed his dream of greatness and security into a simple statement, which statement, implied that his dream of greatness and security was already realized. Then he repeated the statement over and over again to himself until the idea of greatness and security filled his mind and crowded all other ideas out of his consciousness. These may not have been the words of Dr. Millikan but they are those given to me and I quote, "I have a lavish, steady, dependable income, consistent with integrity and mutual benefit." As I have said repeatedly, everything depends upon our attitude towards ourselves. That which we will not affirm as true of ourselves cannot develop in our life. Dr. Millikan wrote his dream of greatness and security in the first person, present tense. He did not say, "I will be great; I will be secure," for that would have implied that he was not great and secure. Instead, he made his future dream a present fact. "I have," said he, "a lavish, steady, dependable income, consistent with integrity and mutual benefit."

The future dream must become a present fact in the mind of him who seeks to realize it. We must experience in imagination what we would experience in reality in the event we achieved our goal, for the soul imagining itself into a situation takes on the results of that imaginary act. If it does not imagine itself into a situation, it is ever free of the result.

It is the purpose of this teaching to lift us to a higher state of consciousness, to stir the highest in us to confidence and self-assertion, for that which stirs the highest in us is our teacher and healer. The very first word of correction or cure is always, "Arise." If we are to understand the reason for this constant command of the Bible to "arise," we must recognize that the universe understood internally is an infinite series of levels and man is what he is according to where he is in that series. As we are lifted up in consciousness, our world reshapes itself in harmony with the level to which we are lifted. He who raises from his prayer a better man, his prayer has been granted.

To change the present state we, like Dr. Millikan, must rise to a higher level of consciousness. This rise is accomplished by affirming that we are already that which we want to be; by assuming the feeling of the wish fulfilled. The drama of life is a psychological one which we bring to pass by our attitudes rather than by our acts. There is no escape from our present predicament except by a radical psychological transformation. Everything depends upon our attitude towards ourselves. That which we will not affirm as true of ourselves will not develop in our lives.

We hear much of the humble man, the meek man – but what is meant by a meek man? He is not poor and groveling, the proverbial doormat, as he is generally conceived to be. Men who make themselves as worms in their own sight have lost the vision of that life – into the likeness of which it is the true purpose of the spirit to transform this life. Men should take their measurements not from life as they see it but from men like Dr. Millkan, who, while poor and unproven, dared to assume, "I have a lavish, steady, dependable income, consistent with integrity and mutual benefit." Such men are the meek of the Gospels, the men who inherit the earth. Any concept of self less than the best robs us of the earth. The promise is, "Blessed are the meek, for they shall inherit the earth." In the original text, the word translated as meek is the opposite of the words – resentful – angry. It has the meaning of becoming "tamed" as a wild animal is tamed. After the mind is tamed, it may be likened to a vine, of which it may be said, "Behold this vine. I found it a wild tree whose wanton strength had swollen into irregular twigs. But I pruned the plant, and it grew temperate in its vain expense of useless leaves, and knotted as you see into these clean, full clusters to repay the hand that wisely wounded it."

A meek man is a self-disciplined man. He is so disciplined he sees only the finest, he thinks only the best. He is the one who fulfills the suggestion, "Brethren, whatsoever things are true, whatsoever things are honest, whatsoever things are just, whatsoever things are pure, whatsoever things are lovely, whatsoever things are of good report; if there be any virtue and if there be any praise, think on these things."

We rise to a higher level of consciousness, not because we have curbed our passions, but because we have cultivated our virtues. In truth, a meek man is a man in complete control of his moods, and his moods are the highest, for he knows he must keep a high mood if he would walk with the highest.

It is my belief that all men can, like Dr. Millikan, change the course of their lives. I believe that Dr. Millikan's technique of making his desire a present fact to himself is of great importance to any seeker after the "truth." It is also his high purpose to be of "mutual benefit" that is inevitably the goal of us all. It is much easier to imagine the good of all than to be purely selfish in our imagining. By our imagination, by our affirmations, we can change our world, we can change our future. To the man of high purpose, to the disciplined man, this is a natural measure, so let us all become disciplined men. Next Sunday morning, July 15th, I am speaking as the guest of Dr. Bailes at 10:30 at the Fox-Wilshire Theater on Wilshire Boulevard, near La Cienega. My subject for next Sunday is "Changing Your Future." It is a subject near to the hearts of us all. I hope you will all come on Sunday to learn how to be the disciplined man, the meek man, who "changes his future" to the benefit of his fellow man. If you are observant, you will notice the swift echo or response to your every mood in this message and you will be able to key it to the circumstances of your daily life. When we are certain of the relationship of mood to circumstance in our lives, we welcome what befalls us. We know that all we meet is part of ourselves. In the creation of a new life we must begin at the beginning, with a change of mood. Every high mood of man is the opening of the door to a higher level for him. Let us mould our lives about a high mood or a community of high moods. Individuals, as well as communities, grow spiritually in proportion as they rise to a higher ideal. If their ideal is lowered, they sink to its depths; if their ideal is exalted, they are elevated to heights unimagined. We must keep the high mood if we would walk with the highest; the heights, also, were meant for habitation. All forms of the creative imagination imply elements of feeling. Feeling is the ferment without which no creation is possible. There is nothing wrong with our desire to transcend our present state. There would be no progress in this world were it not for man's dissatisfaction with himself. It is natural for us to seek a more beautiful personal life; it is right that we wish for greater understanding, greater health, greater security. It is stated in the sixteenth chapter of the Gospel of St. John, "Heretofore have ye asked for nothing in my name; ask and ye shall receive, that your joy may be full."

A spiritual revival is needed for mankind, but by spiritual revival I mean a true religious attitude, one in which each individual, himself, accepts the challenge of embodying a new and higher value of himself as Dr. Millikan did. A nation can exhibit no greater wisdom in the mass than it generates in its units. For this reason, I have always preached self-help, knowing that if we strive passionately after this kind of self-help, that is, to embody a new and higher concept of ourselves, then all other kinds of help will be at our service.

The ideal we serve and hope to achieve is ready for a new incarnation; but unless we offer it human parentage it is incapable of birth. We must affirm that we are already that which we hope to be and live as though we were, knowing like Dr. Millikan, that our assumption, though false to the outer world, if persisted in, will harden into fact.

The perfect man judges not after appearances; he judges righteously. He sees himself and others as he desires himself and them to be. He hears what he wants to hear. He sees and hears only the good. He knows the truth, and the truth sets him free and leads him to good. The truth shall set all mankind free. This is our spiritual revival. Character is largely the result of the direction and persistence of voluntary attention.

"Think truly, and thy thoughts shall the world's famine feed;

Speak truly, and each word of thine shall be a fruitful seed;

Live truly, and thy life shall be a great and noble creed."

2. BY IMAGINATION WE BECOME

How many times have we heard someone say, "Oh, it's only his imagination?" Only his imagination – man's imagination is the man himself. No man has too little imagination, but few men have disciplined their imagination. Imagination is itself indestructible. Therein lies the horror of its misuse. Daily, we pass some stranger on the street and observe him muttering to himself, carrying on an imaginary argument with one not present. He is arguing with vehemence, with fear or with hatred, not realizing that he is setting in motion, by his imagination, an unpleasant event which he will presently encounter.

The world, as imagination sees it, is the real world. Not facts, but figments of the imagination, shape our daily lives. It is the exact and literal minded who live in a fictitious world. Only imagination can restore the Eden from which experience has driven us out. Imagination is the sense by which we perceived the above, the power by which we resolve vision into being. Every stage of man's progress is made by the exercise of the imagination. It is only because men do not perfectly imagine and believe that their results are sometimes uncertain when they might always be perfectly certain. Determined imagination is the beginning of all successful operation. The imagination, alone, is the means of fulfilling the intention. The man who, at will, can call up whatever image he pleases is, by virtue of the power of his imagination, least of all subject to caprice. The solitary or captive can, by intensity of imagination and feeling, affect myriads so that he can act through many men and speak through many voices. "We should never be certain," wrote William Butler Yeats in his Ideas of Good and Evil, "that it was not some woman treading in the wine-press who began that subtle change in men's minds, or that the passion did not begin in the mind of some shepherd boy, lighting up his eyes for a moment before it ran upon its way."

Let me tell you the story of a very dear friend of mine, at the time the costume designer of the Music Hall in New York. She told me, one day, of her difficulty in working with one of the producers who invariably criticized and rejected her best work unjustly; that he was often rude and seemed deliberately unfair to her. Upon hearing her story, I reminded her, as I am reminding you, that men can only echo to us that which we whisper to them in secret. I had no doubt but that she silently argued with the producer, not in the flesh, but in quiet moments to herself. She confessed that she did just that each morning as she walked to work. I asked her to change her attitude toward him, to assume that he was congratulating her on her fine designs and she, in turn, was thanking him for his praise and kindness. This young designer took my advice and as she walked to the theater, she imagined a perfect relationship of the producer praising her work and she, in turn, responding with gratitude for his appreciation. This she did morning after morning and in a very short while, she discovered for herself that her own attitude determined the scenery of her existence. The behavior of the producer completely reversed itself. He became the most pleasant professional employer she had encountered. His behavior merely echoed the changes that she had whispered within herself. What she did was by the power of imagination. Her fantasy led his; and she, herself, dictated to him the discourse they eventually had together at the time she was seemingly walking alone.

Let us set ourselves, here and now, a daily exercise of controlling and disciplining our imagination. What finer beginning than to imagine better than the best we know for a friend. There is no coal of character so dead that it will not glow and flame if but slightly turned. Don't blame; only resolve. Life, like music, can by a new setting turn all its discords into harmonies. Represent your friend to yourself as already expressing that which he desires to be. Let us know that with whatever attitude we approach another, a similar attitude approaches us.

How can we do this? Do what my friend did. To establish rapport, call your friend mentally. Focus your attention on him and mentally call his name just as you would to attract his attention were you to see him on the street. Imagine that he has answered, mentally hear his voice – imagine that he is telling you of the great good you have desired for him. You, in turn, tell him of your joy in witnessing his good fortune. Having mentally heard that which you wanted to hear, having thrilled to the news heard, go about your daily task. Your imagined conversation must awaken what it affirmed; the acceptance of the end wills the means. And the wisest reflection could not devise more effective means than those which are willed by the acceptance of the end.

However, your conversation with your friend must be in a manner which does not express the slightest doubt as to the truth of what you imagine that you hear and say. If you do not control your imagination, you will find that you are hearing and saying all that you formerly heard and said. We are creatures of habit; and habit, though not law, acts like the most compelling law in the world. With this knowledge of the power of imagination, be as the disciplined man and transform your world by imagining and feeling only what is lovely and of good report. The beautiful idea you awaken in yourself shall not fail to arouse its affinity in others. Do not wait four months for the harvest. Today is the day to practice the control and discipline of your imagination. Man is only limited by weakness of attention and poverty of imagination. The great secret is a controlled imagination and a well sustained attention, firmly and repeatedly focused on the object to be accomplished.

"Now is the acceptable time to give beauty for ashes, joy for mourning, praise for the spirit of heaviness; that they might be called trees of righteousness, the planting of the Lord that He might be glorified."

Now is the time to control our imagination and attention. By control, I do not mean restraint by will power but rather cultivation through love and compassion. With so much of the world in discord we cannot possibly emphasize too strongly the power of imaginative love. Imaginative Love, that is my subject next Sunday morning when I shall speak for Dr. Bailes while he is on his holiday. The services will be held as always at the Fox Wilshire Theater on Wilshire Boulevard, near La Cienega at 10:30. "As the world is, so is the individual," should be changed to, "As the individual is so is the world." And I hope to be able to bring to each of you present the true meaning of the words of Zechariah, "Speak ye every man the truth to his neighbor and let none of you imagine evil in your hearts against his neighbor." What a wonderful challenge to you and to me. "As a man thinketh in his heart so is he." As a man imagines so is he. Hold fast to love in your imagination. By creating an ideal within your mental sphere you can approximate yourself to this "ideal image" till you become one and the same with it, thereby transforming yourself into it, or rather, absorbing its qualities into the very core of your being. Never, never, lose sight of the power that is within you. Imaginative love lifts the invisible into sight and gives us water in the desert. It builds for the soul its only fit abiding place. Beauty, love and all of good report are the garden, but imaginative love is the way into the garden.

Sow an imaginary conversation, you reap an act;

Sow an act, you reap a habit;

Sow a habit, you reap a character;

Sow a character, you reap your destiny.

By imagination, we are all reaping our destinies, whether they be good, bad, or indifferent. Imagination has full power of objective realization and every stage of man's progress or regression is made by the exercise of imagination. I believe with William Blake, "What seems to be, is, to those to whom it seems to be, and is productive of the most dreadful consequences to those to whom it seems to be, even of torments, despair, and eternal death. By imagination and desire we become what we desire to be. Let us affirm to ourselves that we are what we imagine. If we persist in the assumption that we are what we wish to be, we will become transformed into that which we have imagined ourselves to be. We were born by a natural miracle of love and for a brief space of time our needs were all another's care. In that simple truth lies the secret of life. Except by love, we cannot truly live at all. Our parents in their separate individualities have no power to transmit life. So, back we come to the basic truth that life is the offspring of love. Therefore, no love, no life. Thus, it is rational to say that, "God is Love."

Love is our birthright. Love is the fundamental necessity of our life. "Do not go seeking for that which you are. Those who go seeking for love only make manifest their own lovelessness and the loveless never find love. Only the loving find love and they never have to seek for it."

3. ANSWERED PRAYER

Have you ever had a prayer answered? What wouldn't men give just to feel certain that when they pray, something definite would happen. For this reason, I would like to take a little time to see why it is that some prayers are answered and some apparently fall on dry ground. "When ye pray, believe that ye receive, and ye shall receive." Believe that ye receive – is the condition imposed upon man. Unless we believe that we receive, our prayer will not be answered. A prayer – granted – implies that something is done in consequence of the prayer which otherwise would not have been done. Therefore, the one who prays is the spring of action – the directing mind – and the one who grants the prayer. Such responsibility man refuses to assume, for responsibility it seems, is mankind's invisible nightmare.

The whole natural world is built on law. Yet, between prayer and its answer we see no such relation. We feel that God may answer or ignore our prayer, that our prayer may hit the mark or may miss it. The mind is still unwilling to admit that God subjects Himself to His own laws. How many people believe that there is, between prayer and its answer, a relation of cause and effect?

Let us take a look at the means employed to heal the ten lepers as related in the seventeenth chapter of the Gospel of St. Luke. The thing that strikes us in this story is the method that was used to raise their faith to the needful intensity. We are told that the ten lepers appealed to Jesus to "have mercy" on them – that is – to heal them. Jesus ordered them to go and show themselves to the priests, and "as they went, they were cleansed." The Mosaic Law demanded that when a leper recovered from his disease he must show himself to the priest to obtain a certificate of restored health. Jesus imposed a test upon the lepers' faith and supplied a means by which their faith could be raised to its full potency. If the lepers refused to go – they had no faith – and, therefore, could not be healed. But, if they obeyed Him, the full realization of what their journey implied would break upon their minds as they went and this dynamic thought would heal them. So, we read, "As they went, they were cleansed."

You, no doubt, often have heard the words of that inspiring old hymn – "Oh, what peace we often forfeit; oh, what needless pain we bear, all because we do not carry everything to God in prayer." I, myself, came to this conviction through experience, being led to brood upon the nature of prayer. I believe in the practice and philosophy of what men call prayer, but not everything that receives that name is really prayer.

Prayer is the elevation of the mind to that which we seek. The very first word of correction is always "arise." Always lift the mind to that which we seek. This is easily done by assuming the feeling of the wish fulfilled. How would you feel if your prayer were answered? Well, assume that feeling until you experience in imagination what you would experience in reality if your prayer were answered. Prayer means getting into action mentally. It means holding the attention upon the idea of the wish fulfilled until it fills the mind and crowds all other ideas out of the consciousness. This statement that prayer means getting into action mentally and holding the attention upon the idea of the wish fulfilled until it fills the mind and crowds all other ideas out of the consciousness, does not mean that prayer is a mental effort – an act of will. On the contrary, prayer is to be contrasted with an act of will. Prayer is a surrender. It means abandoning oneself to the feeling of the wish fulfilled. If prayer brings no response – there is something wrong with the prayer and the fault lies generally in too much effort. Serious confusion arises insofar as men identify the state of prayer with an act of will, instead of contrasting it with an act of will. The sovereign rule is to make no effort, and if this is observed, you will intuitively fall into the right attitude.

Creativeness is not an act of will, but a deeper receptiveness – a keener susceptibility. The acceptance of the end – the acceptance of the answered prayer – finds the means for its realization. Feel yourself into the state of the answered prayer until the state fills the mind and crowds all other states out of your consciousness. What we must work for is not the development of the will, but the education of the imagination and the steadying of attention. Prayer succeeds by avoiding conflict. Prayer is, above all things, easy. Its greatest enemy is effort. The mighty surrenders itself fully only to that which is most gentle. The wealth of

Heaven may not be seized by a strong will, but surrenders itself, a free gift, to the God-spent moment. Along the lines of least resistance travel spiritual as well as physical forces.

We must act on the assumption that we already possess that which we desire, for all that we desire is already present within us. It only waits to be claimed. That it must be claimed is a necessary condition by which we realize our desires. Our prayers are answered if we assume the feeling of the wish fulfilled and continue in that assumption. One of the loveliest examples of an answered prayer I witnessed in my own living room. A very charming lady from out of town came to see me concerning prayer. As she had no one with whom to leave her eight-year old son, she brought him with her the time of our interview. Seemingly, he was engrossed in playing with a toy truck, but at the end of the interview with his mother he said, "Mr. Neville, I know how to pray now. I know what I want – a collie puppy – and I can imagine I am hugging him every night on my bed." His mother explained to him and to me the impossibilities of his prayer, the cost of the puppy, their confined home, even his inability to care for the dog properly. The boy looked into his mother's eyes and simply said, "But, Mother, I know how to pray now." And he did. Two months later during a "Kindness to Animals Week" in his city, all the school children were required to write an essay on how they would love and care for a pet. You have guessed the answer. His essay, out of the five thousand submitted, won the prize, and that prize, presented by the mayor of the city to the lad – was a collie puppy. The boy truly assumed the feeling of his wish fulfilled, hugging and loving his puppy every night.

Prayer is an act of Imaginative Love which is to be the subject of my message next Sunday morning at 10:30 at the Fox Wilshire Theater on Wilshire Boulevard near La Cienega. It is my desire, next Sunday, that I may explain to you, how you, like the young boy; can yield yourselves to the lovely images of your desires and persist in your prayer even though you, like the lad, are told that your desires are impossible.

The necessity of persistence in prayer is shown us in the Bible. "Which of you," asked Jesus, "shall go unto him at midnight, and say unto him: Friend, lend me three loaves; for a friend of mine is come to me from a journey, and I have nothing to set before him; and he from within shall answer and say,

'Trouble me not; the door is now shut and my children are with me in bed; I cannot rise and give thee.' I say unto you, though he will not rise and give him because he is his friend, yet because of his importunity he will arise and give as many as he needeth." Luke 2. The word translated as "importunity" means, literally, shameless impudence. We must persist until we succeed in imagining ourselves into the situation of the answered prayer. The secret of success is found in the word "perseverance." The soul imagining itself into the act, takes on the results of the act. Not imagining itself into the act, it is ever free from the result. Experience in imagination what you would experience in reality were you already what you want to be, and you will take on the result of that act. Do not experience in imagination what you want to experience in reality and you will ever be free of the result. "When ye pray, believe that ye receive, and ye shall receive." One must persist until he reaches his friend on a higher level of consciousness. He must persist until his feeling of the wish fulfilled has all the sensory vividness of reality.

Prayer is a controlled waking dream. If we are to pray successfully, we must steady our attention to observe the world as it would be seen by us were our prayer answered.

Steadying attention makes no call upon any special faculty, but it does demand control of imagination. We must extend our senses – observe our changed relationship to our world and trust this observation. The new world is not there to grasp, but to sense, to touch. The best way to observe it is to be intensely aware of it. In other words, we can, by listening as though we heard and by looking as though we saw, actually hear voices and see scenes from within ourselves that are otherwise not audible or visible. With our attention focused on the state desired, the outer world crumbles and then the world – like music – by a new setting, turns all its discords into harmonies. Life is not a struggle but a surrender. Our prayers are answered by the powers we invoke not by those we exert. So long as the eyes take notice, the soul is blind – for the world that moves us is the one we imagine, not the world round about us. We must yield our whole being to the feeling of being the noble one we want to be. If anything is kept back, the prayer is vain. We often are deprived of our high goal by our effort to possess it. We are called upon to act on the assumption that we already are the man we would be. If we do this without effort – experiencing in imagination what we would experience in the flesh had we realized our goal, we shall find that we do, indeed, possess it. The healing touch is in our attitude. We need change nothing but our attitude towards it. Assume a virtue if you have it not, assume the feeling of your wish fulfilled. "Pray for my soul; more things are wrought by prayer than this world dreams of."

4. MEDITATION

Many people tell me they cannot meditate. This seems to me a bit like saying they cannot play the piano after one attempt. Meditation, as in every art or expression, requires constant practice for perfect results. A truly great pianist, for instance, would feel he could not play his best if he missed one day of practice. If he missed a week or a month of practice he would know that even his most uninitiated audience would recognize his defects. So it is with meditation. If we practice daily with joy in this daily habit, we perfect it as an art. I find that those who complain of the difficulty in meditation do not make it a daily practice, but rather, wait until something pressing appears in their world and then, through an act of will, try to fix their attention on the desired state. But they do not know that meditation is the education of the will, for when will and imagination are in conflict, imagination invariably wins.

The dictionaries define meditation as fixing one's attention upon; as planning in the mind; as devising and looking forward; engaging in continuous and contemplative thought. A lot of nonsense has been written about meditation. Most books on the subject get the reader nowhere, for they do not explain the process of meditation. All that meditation amounts to is a controlled imagination and a well sustained attention. Simply hold the attention on a certain idea until it fills the mind and crowds all other ideas out of consciousness. The power of attention shows itself the sure guarantee of an inner force. We must concentrate on the idea to be realized, without permitting any distraction. This is the great secret of action. Should the attention wander, bring it back to the idea you wish to realize and do so again and again, until the attention becomes immobilized and undergoes an effortless fixation upon the idea presented to it. The idea must hold the attention – must fascinate it – so to speak. All meditation ends at last with the thinker, and he finds he is what he, himself, has conceived. The undisciplined man's attention is the servant of his vision rather than its master. It is captured by the pressing rather than the important.

In the act of meditation, as in the act of adoration, silence is our highest praise. Let us keep our silent sanctuaries, for in them the eternal perspectives are preserved. Day by day, week by week, year by year, at times where none through love or lesser intentions were allowed to interfere, I set myself to attain mastery over my attention and imagination. I sought out ways to make more securely my own, those magical lights that dawned and faded within me. I wished to evoke them at will and to be the master of my vision.

I would strive to hold my attention on the activities of the day in unwavering concentration so that, not for one moment, would the concentration slacken. This is an exercise – a training for higher adventures of the soul. It is no light labor. The ploughman's labor, working in the fields is easier by far.

Empires do not send legions so swiftly to obstruct revolt as all that is alive in us hurries along the nerve highways of the body to frustrate our meditative mood. The beautiful face of one we love glows before us to enchant us from our task. Old enmities and fears beleaguer us. If we are tempted down these vistas, we find, after an hour of musing, that we have been lured away. We have deserted our task and forgotten that fixity of attention we set out to achieve. What man is there who has complete control of his imagination and attention. A controlled imagination and steadied attention, firmly and repeatedly focused on the idea to be realized, is the beginning of all magical operations. If he persists through weeks and months, sooner or later, through meditation, he creates in himself a center of power. He will enter a path all may travel but on which few do journey. It is a path within himself where the feet first falter in shadow and darkness, but which later is made brilliant by an inner light. There is no need for special gifts or genius. It is not bestowed on any individual but won by persistence and practice of meditation. If he persists, the dark caverns of his brain will grow luminous and he will set out day after day for the hour of meditation as if to keep an appointment with a lover. When it comes, he rises within himself as a diver, too long under water, rises to breathe the air and see the light. In this meditative mood he experiences in imagination what he would experience in reality had he realized his goal, that he may in time become transformed into the image of his imagined state.

The only test of religion worth making is whether it is trueborn; whether it springs from the deepest consciousness of the individual; whether it is the fruit of experience; or whether it is anything else whatever. This is my reason for speaking to you on my last Sunday in Los Angeles about The True Religious Attitude. What is your religious attitude? What is my religious attitude? I shall speak on this subject next Sunday morning at 10:30 as Dr. Bailes' guest. The service will be held at the Fox Wilshire Theater on Wilshire Boulevard near La Cienega. I shall endeavor to show you that the methods of mental and spiritual knowledge are entirely different. For we know a thing mentally by looking at it from the outside, by comparing it with other things, by analyzing and defining it; whereas we can know a thing spiritually only by becoming it. We must be the thing itself and not merely talk about it or look at it. We must be in love if we are to know what love is. We must be God-like if we are to know what God is.

Meditation, like sleep, is an entrance into the subconscious. "When you pray, enter into your closet, and when you have shut your door, pray to your Father which is in secret and your Father which is in secret shall reward you openly." Meditation is an illusion of sleep which diminishes the impression of the outer world and renders the mind more receptive to suggestion from within. The mind in meditation is in a state of relaxation akin to the feeling attained just before dropping off to sleep. This state is beautifully described by the poet, Keats, in his ODE TO A NIGHTINGALE. It is said that as the poet sat in the garden and listened to the nightingale, he fell into a state which he described as "A drowsy numbness pains my senses as though of hemlock I had drunk." Then after singing his ode to the nightingale, Keats asked himself this question, "Was it a vision or a waking dream? Fled is the music; do I wake or sleep?" Those are the words of one who has seen something with such vividness or reality that he wonders whether the evidence of his physical eyes can now be believed.

Any kind of meditation in which we withdraw into ourselves without making too much effort to think is an outcropping of the subconscious. Think of the subconscious as a tide which ebbs and flows. In sleep, it is a flood tide, while at moments of full wakefulness, the tide is at its lowest ebb. Between these two extremes are any number of intermediary levels. When we are drowsy, dreamy, lulled in gentle reverie, the tide is high. The more wakeful and alert we become, the lower the tide sinks. The highest tide compatible with the conscious direction of our thoughts occurs just before we fall asleep and just after we wake. An easy way to create this passive state is to relax in a comfortable chair or on a bed. Close your eyes and imagine that you are sleepy, so sleepy, and so very sleepy. Act precisely as though you were going to take a siesta. In so doing, you allow the subconscious tide to rise to sufficient height to make your particular assumption effective.

When you first attempt this, you may find that all sorts of counter-thoughts try to distract you, but if you persist, you will achieve a passive state. When this passive state is reached, think only on "things of good report" – imagine that you are now expressing your highest ideal, not how you will express it, but simply feel Here And Now that you are the noble one you desire to be. You are it now. Call your high ideal into being by imagining and feeling you are it now.

I think all happiness depends on the energy to assume the feeling of the wish fulfilled, to assume the mask of some other more perfect life. If we cannot imagine ourselves different from what we are and try to assume that second more desirable self, we cannot impose a discipline upon ourselves though we may accept discipline from others.

Meditation is an activity of the soul; it is an active virtue; and an active virtue, as distinguished from passive acceptance of a code is theatrical. It is dramatic; it is the wearing of a mask. As your goal is accepted, you become totally indifferent to possible failure, for acceptance of the end wills the means to the end. When you emerge from the moment of meditation it is as though you were shown the happy end of a play in which you are the principal actor. Having witnessed the end in your meditation, regardless of any anti-climatic state you encounter, you remain calm and secure in the knowledge that the end has been perfectly defined.

Creation is finished and what we call creativeness is really only a deeper receptiveness or keener susceptibility on our part, and this receptiveness is "Not by might, nor by power, but by my spirit, saith the Lord of Hosts." Through meditation, we awaken within ourselves a center of light, which will be to us a pillar of cloud by day and a pillar of fire by night.

5. THE LAW OF ASSUMPTION

The great mystic, William Blake, wrote almost two hundred years ago, "What seems to be, is, to those to whom it seems to be and is productive of the most dreadful consequences to those to whom it seems to be." Now, at first, this mystical gem seems a bit involved, or at best to be a play on words; but it is nothing of the kind. Listen to it carefully. "What seems to be, is, to those to whom it seems to be." That is certainly clear enough. It is a simple truth about the law of assumption, and a warning of the consequences of its misuse. The author of the Epistle to the Romans declared in the fourteenth chapter, "I know, and am persuaded by the Lord Jesus, that there is nothing unclean of itself; but to him that esteemeth anything to be unclean, to him it is unclear."

We see by this that it is not superior insight but purblindness that reads into the greatness of men some littleness with which it chances to be familiar, for what seems to be, is, to those to whom it seems to be.

Experiments recently conducted at two of our leading universities revealed this great truth about the law of assumption. They stated in their releases to the newspapers, that after two thousand experiments they came to the conclusion that, 'What you see when you look at something depends not so much on what is there as on the assumption you make when you look. What you believe to be the real physical world is actually only an assumptive world." In other words, you would not define your husband in the same way that you mother would. Yet, you are both defining the same person. Your particular relationship to a thing influences your feelings with respect to that thing and makes you see in it an element which is not there. If your feeling in the matter is a self-element; it can be cast out. If it is a permanent distinction in the state considered, it cannot be cast out. The thing to do is to try. If you can change your opinion of another, then what you now believe of him cannot be absolutely true, but relatively true.

Men believe in the reality of the external world because they do not know how to focus and condense their powers to penetrate its thin crust. Strangely enough, it is not difficult to penetrate this view of the senses. To remove the veil of the senses, we do not employ great effort; the objective world vanishes as we turn our attention from it. We have only to concentrate on the state desired to mentally see it; but to give reality to it so that it will become an objective fact, we must focus our attention upon the desired state until it has all the sensory vividness and feeling of reality. When, through concentrated attention, our desire appears to possess the distinctness and feeling of reality; when the form of thought is as vivid as the form of nature, we have given it the right to become a visible fact in our lives. Each man must find the means best suited to his nature to control his attention and concentrate it on the desired state. I find for myself the best state to be one of meditation, a relaxed state akin to sleep, but a state in which I am still consciously in control of my imagination and capable of fixing my attention on a mental object.

If it is difficult to control the direction of your attention while in this state akin to sleep, you may find gazing fixedly into an object very helpful. Do not look at its surface, but rather into and beyond any plain object such as a wall, a carpet or any object which possesses depth. Arrange it to return as little reflection as possible. Imagine, then, that in this depth you are seeing and hearing what you want to see and hear until your attention is exclusively occupied by the imagined state.

At the end of your meditation, when you awake from your controlled waking dream you feel as though you had returned from a great distance. The visible world which you had shut out returns to consciousness and, by its very presence, informs you that you have been self-deceived into believing that the object of your contemplation was real; but if you remain faithful to your vision this sustained mental attitude will give reality to your visions and they will become visible concrete facts in your world.

Define your highest ideal and concentrate your attention upon this ideal until you identify yourself with it. Assume the feeling of being it – the feeling that would be yours were you now embodying it in your world. This assumption, though now denied by your senses, "if persisted in" – will become a fact in your world. You will know when you have succeeded in fixing the desired state in consciousness simply by looking mentally at the people you know. This is a wonderful check on yourself as your mental conversations are more revealing than your physical conversations are. If, in your mental conversations with others, you talk with them as you formerly did, then you have not changed your concept of self, for all changes of concepts of self result in a changed relationship to the world. Remember what was said earlier, "What you see when you look at something depends not so much on what is there as on the assumption you make when you look." Therefore, the assumption of the wish fulfilled should make you see the world mentally as you would physically were your assumption a physical fact. The spiritual man speaks to the natural man through the language of desire. The key to progress in life and to the fulfillment of dreams lies in the ready obedience to the voice. Unhesitating obedience to its voice is an immediate assumption of the wish fulfilled. To desire a state is to have it. As Pascal said, "You would not have sought me had you not already found me." Man, by assuming the feeling of the wish fulfilled and then living and acting on this conviction changes his future in harmony with his assumption. To "change his future" is the inalienable right of freedom loving individuals. There would be no progress in the world were it not for the divine discontent in man which urges him on to higher and higher levels of consciousness. I have chosen this subject so close to the hearts of us all – "Changing Your Future" – for my message next Sunday morning. I am to have the great joy of speaking for Dr. Bailes while he is vacationing. The service will be held at 10:30 at the Fox Wilshire Theater on Wilshire Boulevard near La Cienega Boulevard.

Since the right to change our future is our birthright as sons of God, let us accept its challenge and learn just how to do it. Again today, speaking of changing your future, I wish to stress the importance of a real transformation of self – not merely a slight alteration of circumstances which, in a matter of moments, will permit us to slip back into the old dissatisfied man. In your meditation, allow others to see you as they would see you were this new concept of self a concrete fact. You always seem to others the embodiment of the ideal you inspire. Therefore, in meditation, when you contemplate others, you must be seen by them mentally as you would be seen by them physically were your conception of yourself an objective fact. That is, in meditation, you imagine that they see you expressing this nobler man you desire to be. If you assume that you are what you want to be, your desire is fulfilled and, in fulfillment, all longing "to be" is neutralized. This, also, is an excellent check on yourself as to whether or not you have actually succeeded in changing self. You cannot continue desiring what has been realized. Rather, you are in a mood to give thanks for a gift received. Your desire is not something you labor to fulfill, it is recognizing something you already possess. It is assuming the feeling of being that which you desire to be.

Believing and being are one. The conceiver and his conception are one. Therefore, that which you conceive yourself to be can never be so far off as even to be near, for nearness implies separation. "If thou canst believe, all things are possible to him that believeth." Faith is the substance of things hoped for, the evidence of things not yet seen. If you assume that you are that finer, nobler one you wish to be, you will see others as they are related to your high assumption. All enlightened men wish for the good of others. If it is the good of another you seek, you must use the same controlled contemplation. In meditation, you must represent the other to yourself as already being or having the greatness you desire for him. As for yourself, your desire for another must be an intense one. It is through desire that you rise above your present sphere and the road from longing to fulfillment is shortened as you experience in imagination all that you would experience in the flesh were you or your friend the embodiment of the desire you have for yourself or him. Experience has taught me that this is the perfect way to achieve my great goals for others as well as for myself. However, my own failures would convict me were I to imply that I have completely mastered the control of my attention. I can, however, with the ancient teacher say: "This one thing I do, forgetting those things which are behind, and reaching forth unto those things which are before – I press towards the mark for the prize."

6. TRUTH

I wish to ask each one of you listening to me today a question – a question which must be close to the hearts of us all concerning truth. If a man known to you as a murderer broke into your home and asked the whereabouts of your mother, would you tell him where she was? Would you tell him the truth? Would you? I venture not – I hope not. In the most mystical of the Gospels – in the Gospel of St. John we read, "Ye shall know the truth, and the truth shall make you free." Therein lies a challenge to us all, "The truth shall make you free." If you told the truth concerning your mother, would you set her free? Again, in John we read, "Sanctify them by the truth." If you gave your mother up to a murderer, would you "sanctify her?" What, then, is the truth of which the Bible so constantly speaks? The truth of the Bible is always coupled with love. The truth of the Bible is that spiritual realization of conscious life in God towards which the human soul evolves through all eternity.

Truth is an ever-increasing illumination. No one who seeks sincerely for truth need fear the outcome for every raising erstwhile truth brings into view some larger truth which it had hidden. The true seeker after truth is not a smug, critical, holier than thou person. Rather, the true seeker after truth knows the words of Zechariah to be true. "Speak ye every man the truth to his neighbor and let none of you imagine evil in your hearts against his neighbor." The seeker after truth does not judge from appearances – he sees the good, the truth in all he observes. He knows that a true judgment need not conform to the external reality to which it relates. Never are we so blind to the truth as when we see things as they seem to be. Only pictures that idealize really depict the truth. It is never superior insight but rather, purblindness that reads into the greatness of another some littleness with which it happens to be familiar.

We all know at least one petty gossip who not only imagines evil against his neighbor, but also insists upon spreading that evil far and wide. His cruel accusations are always accompanied by the statement, "It's a fact," or "I know it's the truth." How far from the truth he is. Even if it were the truth as he knows the truth, it is better not to voice it for "A truth told with bad intent beats all the lies you can invent." Such a man is not a seeker after the truth as revealed in the Bible. He seeks not truth so much as support for his own point of view. By his prejudices, he opens a door by which his enemies enter and make their own the secret places of his heart. Let us seek sincerely for the truth as Robert Browning expresses it:

"Truth is within ourselves; it take no rise

From outward things, whate'er you may believe.

There is an immortal center in us all

Where truth abides in fullness.

The truth that is within us is governed by imaginative love. Knowing this great truth, we can no longer imagine evil against any neighbor. We will imagine the best of our neighbor.

It is my belief that wherever man's attitude towards life is governed by imaginative love, there it is religious – there he worships – there he perceives the truth. I am going to speak on this subject next Sunday morning when my title will be, "Imaginative Love." At that time, I am to have the pleasure and the privilege of taking Dr. Frederick Bailes' service at the Fox Wilshire Theater on Wilshire Boulevard near La Cienega. The service will be held as Dr. Bailes always conducts it at 10:30 Sunday morning.

It is an intuitive desire of all mankind to be a finer, nobler being, to do the loving thing. But we can do the loving thing only when all we imagine is full of love for our neighbor. Then we know the truth, the truth that sets all mankind free. I believe this is a message that will aid us all in the art of living a better and finer life. Infinite love in unthinkable origin was called God, the Father. Infinite love in creative expression was called God, the Son. Infinite love in universal interpenetration, in Infinite Immanence, and in Eternal procession, was called God, the Holy Ghost. We must learn to know ourselves as Infinite Love, as good rather than evil. This is not something that we have to become; it is, rather, for us to recognize something that we are already.

The original birthplace of imagination is in love. Love is its lifeblood. Insofar as imagination retains its own life's blood, its visions are images of truth. Then it mirrors the living identity of the thing it beholds. But if imagination should deny the very power that has brought it to birth then the direst sort of horror will begin. Instead of rendering back living images of the truth, imagination will fly to love's opposite – fear and its visions will then be perverted and contorted reflections cast upon a screen of frightful fantasy. Instead of being the supremely creative power, it will become the active agent of destruction. Wherever man's attitude to life is truly imaginative, there man and God are merged in creative unity. Remember that Love is always creative, causative in every sphere from the highest to the very lowest. There never has existed thought, word or deed that was not caused by love, or by its opposite – fear of some kind, even if it were only a desire of a not very worthy aim. Love and fear are the mainspring of our mental machinery. Everything is a thought before it becomes a thing. I suggest the pursuit of a high ideal to make a fact of being become a fact of consciousness and to do this by training the imagination to realize that the only atmosphere in which we truly live and move and have our being is Infinite Love. God is Love. Love never faileth. Infinite Creative Spirit is Love. The urge that caused Infinite unconditioned consciousness to condition itself into millions of sensitive forms is Love.

Love regarded as an abstraction – apart from an object – is unthinkable. Love is not love if there is no beloved. Love only becomes thinkable in relation, in process in act. Let us recognize with Blake that, "He who will not live by love must be subdued by fear," and set ourselves the highest of ideals to love and to live by. But our highest ideals do not bless unless they come down and take on flesh. We must make results and accomplishments the crucial test of our imagination and our love, for incarnation is the only true realization. Our faithfulness must be to the sum of all the truth we know and it must be absolute. Otherwise, that truth lacks a vehicle and cannot be incarnated in us.

Our concept of ourselves determines the scenery of our lives. We are ever our own jailers. The prison doors that we thought closed are truly ajar – waiting for us to see the truth. "Man ever surrounds himself with the true image of himself," said Emerson. "Every spirit builds itself a house and beyond its house, a world, and beyond its world, a heaven. Know then the world exists for you, for you the phenomenon is perfect. What we are that only can we see. All that Adam had, all the Caesar could, you have and can do."

Adam called his house heaven and earth. Caesar called his house, Rome. You perhaps call yours a cobbler's trade, or a hundred acres of land, or a scholar's garret. Yet line for line, and point for point, your dominion is as great as theirs, though without such fine names. Build, therefore, your own world and as fast as you confirm your life to the pure idea in your mind, that will unfold its great proportions.

The truth is our secret inward reality, the cause, the meaning, the relation of our lives to all things. Let the truth carry us heavenwards, expanding our conceptions, increasing our understanding until we know the "Truth" and are made "Free."

7. STONE, WATER OR WINE?

It has been my privilege and pleasure to address Dr. Frederick Bailes' Sunday audiences in the past few years. Today, I am to extend the privilege in speaking to you, his unseen audience of the radio. This will be a very practical series of talks for my subjects will be drawn largely from the Bible, the most spiritual of all books. And I am firmly convinced that whatever is most profoundly spiritual is, in reality, most directly practical. All mistakes made in Biblical interpretation come from referring statements of which the intention is spiritual and mystical, and implying principles or states to times, persons or places. In one sense, not one work of Scripture is true according to the letter. Yet, I say that every word is true; but the Scriptures are true only as He intended them that spoke them; they are true as God meant them, not as man will have them. A spiritual and symbolical interpretation alone yields truth, whilst a literal acceptation profits nothing. The Bible contains historical elements, but these are always used as picture language of great ideas.

The Gospel narrative is to be studied in order that we may know. It does not convey knowledge immediately.

Getting to know is a gradual process – a progressive inner experience. God reveals Himself within us as we are able to receive Him. The deep meanings have always been recognized partially by a few, as will be found by consulting the writings of the seers of all past ages.

In assigning to the Bible its proper meaning, it is necessary to remember that as mystical Scriptures it deals primarily, not with material things or persons, but with spiritual significations. The Bible is addressed not to the outer sense or reason, but to the soul. Its object is not to give an historical account of physical life, but to exhibit the spiritual possibilities of humanity, at large, for religion is not in its nature historical and dependent upon actual sensible events, but consists in processes such as Faith and Redemption. These, being interior to all men, subsist irrespective of what any particular man has at any time done. The perennial value of the Bible is its symbolic value. There are great controversies as to what is and what is not historical in the Bible, but let us remember that if we could settle all the historical questions tomorrow, that would not give us religion, nor would it give the Bible a biding value. Everything depends upon our finding the symbolical value of the facts. A fact of past history has nothing in it for present day religion unless it stands forth as a symbol of a Reality behind itself.

The Bible is a revelation of Truth expressed in Divine symbolism. From the literal point of view, the wording may sometimes be confusing; it is the symbolism, alone, which is precious and worthy of our best efforts to elucidate. All Scripture was written from the inward mystery and not with a mystical sense put into it. The stories conceal an underlying meaning, and the task of scripture interpretation is to discover these psychological truths which are expressed in this symbolism. We, here, are not concerned with the surface meaning of the Scripture, whether it be reasonable or absurd, for in no case does it constitute the inner truth we are seeking. Throughout the centuries we have mistakenly taken personification for persons, allegory for history, the vehicle that conveyed the instruction for the instruction itself and the gross first sense for the ultimate sense intended. In most of the little things of life, this confusion is of trivial consequence. But the error which arises when you carry the confusion into questions of greater moment, such as religion, assumes gigantic proportions. For centuries, men have sought eagerly for bits of evidence which might be related to the happenings described in the Bible. While most people believe that its characters lived, no proof of their lives on earth has ever been found and may never be found. This is unimportant for the ancient teachers were not writing history, but an allegorical picture lesson of certain basic principles, which they clothed in the garb of history. The form of the various stories of the Bible is as distinct from its substance as the form of a grain of wheat is distinct from the life germ within it. As the assimilative organs of the body discriminate between food that can be built into the physical system and food that must be cast off, so do the awakened intuitive faculties discover, beneath allegory and parable, the psychological life germ, and feeding on this, they cast off the fiction which conveyed it. The Bible is the largest selling book in this country. It is probably the least read and certainly the least understood. Throughout the Bible, the symbols of stone, water and wine are used. The stones of the Bible are its literal truths. The Ten Commandments, we are told, were written on stone. The water of the Bible is the psychological meaning hidden in these literal truths of stone. "I give you living waters," that is, the inner knowledge that can make these stories a living reality in your life. The wine you must make for yourself through the wise use of this living water or psychological truth. This is an absolute necessity to the truly religious man. This is what Sir Walter Scott meant when he said, "Man's greatest education is that which he gives to himself."

On Sunday morning, I shall speak on, "Are You Stone, Water or Wine?" I shall be taking Dr. Bailes' service at 10:30 at the Fox Wilshire Theater on Wilshire Boulevard near La Cienega. When you hear this message, you may ask yourselves, "Are you stone, water or wine?" You may judge whether your understanding of the Bible is merely literal, psychological, or truly spiritual and, therefore, profoundly practical.

The Bible is, from beginning to end, all about transcending the violence which characterizes mankind's present level of being. It affirms the possibility of a development of another level of being surmounting violence. The point of view taken is that the goal of man is this inner development, which is the only real psychology. To take the Bible away from its central idea of rebirth, which means an inner evolution and implies the existence of a higher level, is to understand nothing of its real meaning. The Word of God, that is, the psychological teaching in the Bible, is to make a man different, first in thought and then in being, so that he becomes a new man or is born again.

Whenever an entirely new attitude enters into a person's life, psychological rebirth to some extent has occurred. Man wants to be better, not different. The Bible speaks, not of being better, but of another man, a man reborn. "Except a man be born again, he cannot see the Kingdom of God… Except a man be born of water and the spirit, he cannot enter into the Kingdom of God. Marvel not that I said unto thee, ye must be born again." (John 3.) The Ten Commandments were written on tablets of stone for those incapable of seeing any deeper meaning. Stone represents the most external and literal form of spiritual truth, and water refers to another way of understanding the same truth. Wine or spirit is the highest form of understanding it.

"Such as men themselves are, such will God appear to them to be," wrote John Smith, the Cambridge Platonist. "The God of the moralist is before all things a great judge and schoolmaster; the God of Science is impersonal and inflexible Vital Law; the God of the savage is the kind of chief he would be himself if he had the opportunity." No man's conduct will be higher than his conception of God, and his conception of God is determined by the kind of man he, himself, is. "For such as men themselves are, such will God appear to them to be," and what is true of man's concept of God is equally true of man's concept of God's Word, the Bible. It will be to him what he is to himself.

"God is God from the creation,

Truth alone is man's salvation;

But the God that now you worship

Soon shall be your God no more

For the soul in its unfolding

Evermore its thoughts remolding,

Learns more truly in its progress

How to love and to adore."

8. FEELING IS THE SECRET

Recently, I asked a very successful businessman his formula for success. He laughed and was a little embarrassed. Then he replied, "I guess it's just because I can't conceive of failure. It's nothing that I think about much. It's more a feeling that I have." His statement coincided completely with my own beliefs and experiments. We can think about something forever and never see it in our world, but once let us feel its reality, and we are bound to encounter it. The more intensely we feel, the sooner we will encounter it. We all regard feelings far too much as effects, and not sufficiently as causes of the events of the day. Feeling is not only the result of our conditions of life, it is also the creator of those conditions. We say we are happy because we are well, not realizing that the process will work equally well in the reverse direction. We are well because we are happy. We are all far too undisciplined in our feelings. To be joyful for another is to bless ourselves as well as him. To be angry with another is to punish ourselves for his fault. The distressed mind stays at home though the body travels to the ends of the earth, while the happy mind travels though the body remains at home.

Feeling is the secret of successful prayer, for in prayer, we feel ourselves into the situation of the answered prayer and, then, we live and act upon that conviction. Feeling after Him, as the Bible suggests, is a gradual unfolding of the soul's hidden capacities. Feeling yields in importance to no other. It is the ferment without which no creation is possible. All forms of creative imagination imply elements of feeling. All emotional dispositions whatever may influence the creative imagination. Feeling after Him has no finality. It is an acquisition, increasing in proportion to receptivity, which has not and never will have finality. An idea which is only an idea produces nothing and does nothing. It acts only if it is felt, if it is accompanied by effective feeling. Somewhere within the soul there is a mood which, if found, means wealth, health, happiness to us. The creative desire is innate in man. His whole happiness is involved in this impulse to create. Because men do not perfectly "feel," the results of their prayers are unsure, when they might be perfectly sure. We read in Proverbs, "A merry heart doeth good like a medicine but a broken spirit drieth the bones." Orchestral hearts burn in the oil of the lamp of the king. The spirit sings unto the Lord a new song. All true prayer wears a glad countenance; the good are anointed with the oil of gladness above their fellows. Let us, then, watch our feelings, our reactions to the day's events. And let us guard our feelings even more zealously in the act of prayer, for prayer is the true creative state. Dignity indicates that man hears the greater music of life, and moves to the tempo of its deeper meaning. If we did nothing but imagine and feel the lovely, the world's reform would, at once, be accomplished. Many of the stories of the Bible deal exclusively with the power of imagination and feeling. "Feeling after Him" is the cry of the truth seeker. Only imagination and feeling can restore the Eden from which experience has driven us. Feeling and imagination are the senses by which we perceive the beyond. Where knowledge ends, they begin. Every noble feeling of man is the opening for him of some door to the divine world. Let us measure men, not by the height of their cities, but by the magnificence of their imaginations and feelings. Let us turn our thought up to Heaven and mix our imagination with the angels. The world that moves us is the one we imagine, not the world that surrounds us. In the imagination lie the unexplored continents, and man's great future adventure. This consciousness of non-finality in "feeling after God" has been the experience of all earnest God-ward feelers. They realize that their conception of the Infinite has constantly deepened and expanded with experience. Those who endeavor to think out the meaning of the experience and to coordinate it with the rest of our knowledge, are the philosophic mystics; those who try to develop the faculty in themselves, and to deepen the experience are the practical or experimental mystics. Some, and among them the greatest, have tried to do both. Religion begins in subjective experience. Religion is what a man does with his solitude, for in solitude we are compelled to subjective experience.

It is of the Religious Attitude that I shall speak next Sunday morning. This will be the last Sunday morning I shall take the service for Dr. Bailes this season. The service is held at 10:30 at the Fox Wilshire Theater on Wilshire Boulevard, near La Cienega. A True Religious Attitude is man's salvation. God never changes; it is we who are changing; our spiritual eyes are ever getting keener; and this enlargement of truth will bring us an ever-increasing inner peace.

The best defense against the deceptive assault upon our mental and moral eyesight is the spiritual eye or the Eye of God. In other words, a spiritual ideal that cannot be changed by circumstance, a code of personal honor and integrity in ourselves and good will and love to others. "Not what thou art, nor what thou hast been, beholdeth God with his merciful eyes, but that thou wouldst be." Through the veins of the humblest man on earth runs the royal blood of being. Therefore, let us look at man through the eyes of imaginative love which is really seeing with the Eye of God. Under the influence of the Eye of God, the ideal rises up out of the actual as water is etherealized by the sun into the imagery cloudland. Things altogether distant are present to the spiritual eye. The Eye of God makes the future dream a present fact. Not four months to harvest – look again, If we persist in this seeing, one day we will arise with the distance in our eyes, and all the staying, stagnant nearby will suddenly be of no importance. We will brush it aside as we pass on to our far- seen objective. The man who really finds himself cannot do otherwise than let himself be guided by love. He is of too pure eyes to behold iniquity. Our ability to help others will be in proportion to our ability to control and help ourselves. The day a man achieves victory over himself, history will discover that to have been a victory over his enemy. The healing touch is in an attitude, and one day man will discover that one governs souls only with serenity. The mighty surrenders itself fully only to the most gentle.

Recognizing the power of feeling, let us pay strict attention to our moods and attitudes. Every stage of man's progress is made through the exercise of his imagination and feeling. By creating an "ideal" within our mental sphere we can feel ourselves into this "ideal image" till we become one and the same with it, absorbing its qualities into the very core of our being. The solitary or captive can, by the intensity of his imagination and feeling, effect myriads so that he can act through many men and speak through many voices. Extend your feelers, trust your touch, participate in all flights of your imaginations and be not afraid of your own sensitivities. The best way to feel another's good is to be more intensely aware of it. Be like my friend and have "more of a feeling" for the health, the wealth, the happiness you desire. Ideas do not bless unless they descend from Heaven and take flesh. Make results or accomplishments the crucial test of true imagination. As you observe these results, you will determine to fill your images with love and to walk in a high and noble mood for you will know with the poet:

"That which ye sow ye reap.

See yonder fields

The sesamum was sesamum, the corn

Was corn. The Silence and the Darkness knew

So is man's fate born."

9. AFFIRM THE REALITY OF OUR OWN GREATNESS

In the creation of a new way of life, we must begin at the beginning, with our own individual regeneration. The formation of organizations, political bodies, religious bodies, social bodies is not enough. The trouble we see goes deeper than we perceive. The essential revolution must happen within ourselves. Everything depends on our attitude towards ourself – that which we will not affirm within ourself can never develop in our world. This is the religion by which we live, for religion begins in subjective experience, like charity, it begins at home. "Be ye transformed by the renewing of your mind" is the ancient formula and there is no other. Everything depends upon man's attitude toward himself. That which he cannot or will not claim as true of himself can never evolve in his world. Man is constantly looking about his world and asking, "What's to be done? What will happen?" when he should ask himself "Who am I? What is my concept of myself?" If we wish to see the world a finer, greater place, we must affirm the reality of a finer, greater being within ourselves. It is the ultimate purpose of my teaching to point the road to this consummation. I am trying to show you how the inner man must readjust himself – what must be the new premise of his life, in order that he may lose his soul on the level he now knows and find it again on the high level he seeks.

It is impossible for man to see other than the contents of his own consciousness, for nothing has existence for us save through the consciousness we have of it. The ideal man is always seeking a new incarnation but unless we, ourselves, offer him human parentage, he is incapable of birth. We are the means whereby the redemption of nature from the law of cruelty is to be effected. The great purpose of consciousness is to effect this redemption. If we decline the burden and point to natural law as giving us conclusive proof that redemption of the world by imaginative love is something that can never come about, we simply nullify the purpose of our lives through want of faith. We reject the means, the only means, whereby this process of redemption must be effected.

The only test of religion worth making is whether it is trueborn – whether it springs from the deepest conviction of the individual, whether it is the fruit of inner experience. No religion is worthy of a man unless it gives him a deep and abiding sense that all is well, quite irrespective of what happens to him personally. The methods of mental and of spiritual knowledge are entirely different, for we know a thing mentally by looking at it from the outside, by comparing it with other things by analyzing and defining it. Whitehead has defined religion as that which a man does with his solitude. I should like to add, I believe it is what a man is in his solitude. In our solitude we are driven to subjective experience. It is, then, that we should imagine ourselves to be the ideal man we desire to see embodied in the world. If, in our solitude, we experience in our imagination what we would experience in reality had we achieved our goal, we will in time, become transformed into the image of our ideal. "Be renewed in the spirit of your mind – put on the new man – speak every man truth with his neighbor." The process of making a "Fact of being a fact of consciousness" is by the "renewing of our mind." We are told to change our thinking. But we can't change our thought unless we change our ideas. Our thoughts are the natural outpouring of our ideas, and our innermost ideas are the man himself. The end of longing is always to be – not to do. Be still and know "I am that which I desire." Strive always after being. External reforms are useless if your heart is not reformed. Heaven is entered not by curbing our passions; but rather, by cultivating our virtues. An old idea is not fickly forgotten, it is crowded out by new ideas. It disappears when a wholly new and absorbing idea occupies our attention. Old habits of thinking and feeling – like dead oak leaves – hang on till they are pushed off by new ones. Creativeness is basically a deeper receptiveness, a keener susceptibility. The future dream must become a present fact in the mind of anyone who would alter his life. Every great out-picturing is preceded by a period of profound absorption. When that absorption is filled with our highest ideal, – when we become that ideal – then we see it manifest in our world and we realize that the present does not recede into the past, but advances into the future. This is essentially how we change our future. A "now" which is "elsewhere" has for us no absolute meaning. We only recognize "now" when it is at the same time "here." When we feel ourselves into the desired state "here" and "now" we have truly changed our future. It is this "Changing Your Future" which I hope to explain to you fully next Sunday morning when I am speaking for Dr. Bailes at 10:30 at the Fox Wilshire Theater on Wilshire Boulevard near La Cienega. It is my purpose to stir you to a higher concept of yourself and to explain so clearly the method by which you can achieve this concept that each one of you will leave the service on Sunday morning a transformed being.

Discouraged people are sorely in need of the inspiration of great principles. We must get back to first principles if we are to speak with a voice that will kindle the imagination and rouse the spirit. Again, I must repeat, in the creation of a new way of life, we must begin at the very beginning with our own individual regeneration. Man's chief delusion is his conviction that he can do anything. Everyone thinks he can do – everyone wants to do and all ask, "What to do?" What to do? It is impossible to do anything. One must be. It is hard for us to accept the fact that "We, of ourselves, do nothing." It is especially difficult because it is the truth and the truth is always difficult for man to accept. But, actually, nobody can do anything. Everything happens – all that befalls man – all that is done by him – all that comes from him – all this happens, and it happens in exactly the same way that rain falls – as a result of a change in the temperature in the higher regions of the atmosphere. This is a challenge to us all. What concept are we holding of ourselves in the higher regions of our soul?

Everything depends upon man's attitude towards himself. That which he will not affirm as true within himself can never develop in his world. A change of concept of self is the right adjustment – the new relationship between the surface and the depth of man. Deepening is, in principle, always possible, for the ultimate depth lives in everyone, and it is only a question of becoming conscious of it. Life demands of us the willingness to die and to be born again. This is not meant that we die in the flesh. We die in the spirit of the old man to become the new man, then we see the new man in the flesh. "Subjection to the will of God" is an old phrase for it and there is, I believe, no new one that is better. In that self-committal to the ideal we desire to express, all conflict is dispersed and we are transformed into the image of the ideal in whom we rest. We are told that the man without a wedding garment reaches the Kingdom by cleverly pretending. He does not believe internally what he practices externally. He appears good, kind, charitable. He uses the right words, but inwardly he believes nothing. Coming into the strong light of those far more conscious than himself, he ceases to deceive. A wedding garment signifies a desire for union. He has no desire to unite with what he teaches, even if what he teaches is the truth. Therefore, he has no wedding garment. When we are united with the truth, then we will put off the old nature and be renewed in the spirit of our mind.

Truth will strip the clever pretenders of their false aristocracy. Truth, in its turn, will be conquered and governed by the aristocracy of goodness, the only unconquerable thing in the world.

www.ingramcontent.com/pod-product-compliance
Lightning Source LLC
LaVergne TN
LVHW101932220826
846093LV00009B/434
* 9 7 8 9 3 9 0 5 7 5 1 1 4 *